PROUD TO BE A

# Colored

# GIRL

Thank you so
Very Much!
Carolee Colats
2009'
Modeling
Renewal

PROUD TO BE A

# Colored
# GIRL

# JACKIE CHRISTIE

INFINITE L♥VE
publishing
REDMOND, WA

ISBN: 978-0-9794827-6-2
Library of Congress Control Number: 2009920069

Printed in the United States of America
Book cover and interior design by Dotti Albertine | www.AlbertineBookDesign.com
Cover image by D. Tucker
Cover photo of author by Roy Wilcox Photography
Book images by Fotalia and Jupiter Image
Interior photographs by John Hong | www.jkhphotography.com

*I dedicate this book to my loving family,*
*And all the beautiful colored girls in the world!*

# Contents

# Still I Rise

BY MAYA ANGELOU[1]

You may write me down in history
With your bitter, twisted lies,
You may trod me in the very dirt
But still, like dust, I'll rise.

Does my sassiness upset you?
Why are you beset with gloom?
'Cause I walk like I've got oil wells
Pumping in my living room.

Just like moons and like suns,
With the certainty of tides,
Just like hopes springing high,
Still I'll rise.

Did you want to see me broken?
Bowed head and lowered eyes?
Shoulders falling down like teardrops.
Weakened by my soulful cries.

Does my haughtiness offend you?
Don't you take it awful hard
'Cause I laugh like I've got gold mines
Diggin' in my own back yard.

You may shoot me with your words,
You may cut me with your eyes,
You may kill me with your hatefulness,
But still, like air, I'll rise.

Does my sexiness upset you?
Does it come as a surprise
That I dance like I've got diamonds
At the meeting of my thighs?

Out of the huts of history's shame
I rise

Up from a past that's rooted in pain
I rise

I'm a black ocean, leaping and wide,
Welling and swelling I bear in the tide.
Leaving behind nights of terror and fear
I rise

Into a daybreak that's wondrously clear
I rise

Bringing the gifts that my ancestors gave,
I am the dream and the hope of the slave.

I rise

I rise

I rise.

# Acknowledgments

I thank …

God, for everything is possible through Him.

My Husband, my soul mate and the love of my life!

My Children, you are my beautiful angels and I love you.

My parents, thank you for all that you are
   and always have been to me.

Norma Jean, I miss you so very much.

My Family, I love every single one of you.

My friends, you all enrich my life, thank you.

Betty Jones, may you forever rest in peace.

Jade Goody, you are a true inspiration.

Maya Angelou for your beautiful poetry and inspiration.

Barack and Michelle Obama, you both inspire me.

Tyler Perry for being a voice.

Mike Tharpe, a friend for life.

Dotti Albertine, you are just so awesome, Dotti.

Michael Levin, thank you friend for your wisdom.

William Ayers, thanks for the inspiration.

Ty Pollard, what would we do without you T?

Shane Geis, your friendship is beautiful.

D. Tucker, you're the best!

Bobby Tinsley for the beautiful song, "Colored Girl".

Khalid Winston for everything.

And you, the reader, for taking time to experience
   *Proud To Be A Colored Girl!*

*You are truly beautiful.*
—JACKIE CHRISTIE

# Introduction

The age old stereotyping of African American women has gone on practically unchallenged for centuries and probably would continue except we are about to embark upon a journey together, that will explore a different way of thinking and feeling. We'll explore having different perceptions of what has been taught to us and what we have come to accept.

I mean let's face it, how often have you heard the word colored girl? And thought to yourself that it sounded like a racial slur! Well, I'm here to tell you that way of thinking is gone forever! Not only is a colored girl a beautiful person, she is loving and caring and confident in herself. She walks with her head held high and her chest pushed forward exploding with pride, for she is beautiful not just in looks but inside!

The truth is all women, no matter what their nationalities are, have color in their skin. That is a fact! Be it black, brown, white, tan—this, my friend, is "color". Even though we speak different languages and live totally different lifestyles, still if our skin was stripped from our flesh, we would find that we are all the same—a female species, beautiful colored girls.

My favorite poet is Dr. Maya Angelou, and she once said in one of her beautiful poems: **"It's in the reach of my arms, the span of my hips, the stride of my step, the curl of my lips. I'm a woman Phenomenally. Phenomenal woman that's me."** That's all of us, all of us beautiful colored girls!

*Appreciate what others do for you.*

—JACKIE CHRISTIE

# CHAPTER 1

# *Skin Deep*

**Let's talk science and the makeup of the human body …**

The human body's chemical composition consists of a variety of elements and compounds. By mass, human cells consist of 65–90% water ($H_2O$), and a significant portion is composed of carbon-containing organic molecules. Oxygen therefore contributes a majority of a human body's mass, followed by carbon. 99% of the mass of the human body is made up of the six elements oxygen, carbon, hydrogen, nitrogen, calcium, and phosphorus.[2]

Now you may be asking why the lesson in science, right? Well, because in order to understand the female body all the way to the pigment in the skin, we must first go to the root of our being.

We have to ask ourselves the million-dollar question, "Are we really more alike than previously believed?"

Yes we are! Science shows this as well as a basic understanding that all women are human, and all women are females. And, lastly, if our skin was stripped from our bodies, we would be unrecognizable as different races. So in essence we are all very much alike! There is a stigma that comes with the word "colored girl", and we will set out to destroy it. I want you to open your mind and heart and accept that you're a beautiful colored girl. I'm a beautiful colored girl. She is a beautiful colored girl! All of us are. And always will be.

The age old stereotyping about race is just that! Age old. It has no place in our society. All of us here on earth come from very racially diverse cultures. Yet we are (or aspire to be) united in spirit. We can begin now to change some old views and thought processes. We can alter the perception of those who still choose to see color lines. We can be the change!

Dare to step up and love your sisters from all over the world and embrace the differences of cultures and history to find that each woman's inner core is the same as yours—beautiful and kind, caring and pure. We cannot choose our parents, where or the circumstances to which we were born. We can only accept who and what we are now. Also, we have the power to change many or most situations in our lives that make us unhappy, but no power at all to change other people. They must want the change and be open to taking action themselves.

The makeup of a beautiful colored girl is:

— *Her wisdom*
— *Her strength*
— *Her soul*
— *Her honesty*
— *Her pride*
— *Her self respect*
— *Her smile*
— *Her inner beauty*
— *Her heart*
— *Her soul*
— *Her willingness to accept others*
— *Her caring ways*
— *Her conscience*
— *Her confidence*

And her ability to erase any color lines.

# *Just One*
## By Anonymous[3]

One song can spark a moment,
One flower can wake the dream.
One tree can start a forest,
One bird can herald spring.
One smile begins a friendship,
One handclasp lifts a soul.
One star can guide a ship at sea,
One word can frame the goal
One vote can change a nation,
One sunbeam lights a room
One candle wipes out darkness,
One laugh will conquer gloom.
One step must start each journey.
One word must start each prayer.
One hope will raise our spirits,
One touch can show you care.
One voice can speak with wisdom,
One heart can know what's true,
One life can make a difference,
You see, it's up to you!

*Never stop trying to learn.*
—Jackie Christie

CHAPTER 2

# Beautiful Little Girl

*I arise in the morning torn between a desire to improve the world and a desire to enjoy the world. This makes it hard to plan the day.*
—E. B. WHITE

Can you remember being a little girl and going to school for the very first time? Close your eyes for a moment and try to think back to walking in your kindergarten classroom and sitting down for the first time only to feel the eyes of all your classmates looking at you! Was that a good feeling or not so good? Maybe you wondered to yourself why are they all staring at me? Do I look weird in my new shoes and dress? Is my hair out of place? What's going on?

Well welcome to my childhood. Welcome to what I experienced as a little girl going to school in Seattle, Washington. I never really asked any of the kids what they were looking at. I Just tried not to stand out in any way that would provoke that awkward, silent stare again from any of them, because at that time I really didn't understand that the differences in our skin tone made kids feel insecure.

I did make a few new friends though. One was a beautiful, dark-skinned girl named Stephanie. She had long, shiny, black hair and a pretty smile. Plus, she had a really cool older sis named Anisette, and I had an older sis named Tami. Actually I had three older sisters, but Tami was her sister's same age. So, Tami and Anisette eventually became good friends too!

My other close girlfriend in kindergarten was a soft-spoken, beautiful, African-American girl named Mona. She was the quietest of the three of us, and she would always try to keep the peace at school between all the kids. Stephanie and Mona were my crew! Shortly after I began attending the elementary school with them, we were inseparable! We played at lunch together, walked to school together, and even talked about growing up someday and getting our first apartments next door to each other! We would often find ourselves being scolded by the teacher while engulfed in one of our fantasy discussions about the color schemes we would have in our new apartments when we grew up. LOL! We were in kindergarten after all! But we dreamed nonetheless!

However, these fond memories were just a part of my childhood. I also have dark ones. Like the first time I was called the "N" word! I was horrified! I mean, I had seen it on television and heard the stories sometimes while eavesdropping on the grown-ups talking, but never was it directed at me! When I was called this name I felt so hurt, so upset. I wanted to scream at the kid who said it, to tell him to get away from me! And never talk to me again! Because I never saw any differences in our colors before that day. I felt we were all the same on the inside! So the tone of our skin was not important. I couldn't understand why they saw "me" as someone different.

But I also knew that the "N" word was associated with bad, hateful, racist things, and I knew at an early age that I did not want to go through life hating people for the color of their skin, or treating people differently because they were another nationality, or because they were from a different culture. I knew that God created us all as one species and that was *human*. I vowed that no matter how others behaved, I would always treat people with love and try to be the best example of a person who saw no color lines.

I always knew I would grow into a woman someday, and I would have children of my own, and I would teach them to love people no matter what their race, culture, or socioeconomic background was.

I would lead by example and show others that hate has no place in the world. I would demonstrate that even though people called you names or said mean things about you, still you must forgive them. Life is a beautiful gift and we must all appreciate it and cherish it and each other! For all women are beautiful, loving, colored girls!

*Forgiveness is a gift you give yourself.*
—SUZANNE SOMERS

*The art of dance is the art of beauty.*
—JACKIE CHRISTIE

# CHAPTER 3

# A Diamond in the Rough

Deep in every woman's core is a powerful, inner beauty and strength. From that center she has the capacity to command love and respect from men as well as other women. Every woman does possess a strong sense of self, even if she's not yet aware of it.

Inside every woman there is deep love, just waiting to be shared with a special person, anxious to give all of herself to someone, sometimes paying a heavy price for it. But still she is willing to share her soul. It has been said that beauty is only skin deep, but I feel true beauty comes from the inside. I have laid eyes on women across this country, who may not possess a fashion model's features, but have the potential to shine like the brightest star and command the attention of every single male in the room just by her style and grace, and her inner beauty alone. So never discount any woman, for she may really be just a *diamond in the rough* waiting to be revealed.

Growing up I was considered a tomboy. Funny, in looking back, I always knew I was a diamond in the rough! Just waiting to be revealed. I could see how the boys would look at me and flirt, and I would pretend to be tough, and act as though they were the *furthest* things from my mind. When really I thought about them as often as they probably thought about me, but I could never let them in on that secret! Not until, of course, I began to reach puberty and well … you know the buds of breasts began to form and my behind got a little bit bigger and rounder. Suddenly I couldn't pretend to be one of the boys anymore! That's when I realized I was really a girl, in every since of the word! Although, I liked being feminine, I was extremely shy about my body, and told myself it was not the end of the world, I decided that somehow I would get through it, and that I would be able to hide the fact that my curves had a mind of their own, and that I was every bit the female that the boys admired.

At the same time that I was experiencing these changes, my girlfriends were also going through the same thing, except they were not embarrassed about their bodies. They loved all the new curves and the excitement of the attention. Each day was a new day to see if they could drive the boys crazy and you know what? It worked like magic every time. I would, on the other hand, go home and think to myself how silly it was that the girls seemed to accept the fact that we were changing into young women. We were being stared at in a sexual sort of way that should have made them feel uncomfortable too! But not *those* girls!

Well it wasn't too long before we all reached high school, and things were changing quickly! We were all getting more comfortable in our own skin, and we were noticing the boys now too! This was something I thought I would never feel. Much of the time we were trying to look our best and flirting with the boys. We still behaved like *nice* girls, but not to the point of shying away from the advances of a boy we were attracted to.

It wasn't until I joined the African dance ensemble that I really became comfortable with my hips and the roundness of my behind as well as the perkiness of my breasts. While learning African dance I was taught to move and sway the way they dance in the great land of Africa! I learned to move with the rhythm and beat of the drums, and to feel the way in which the music moves your soul. They taught us that every one of us, every nationality that joined the group was beautiful and we were all the same. There were no color lines drawn and we just danced. We could move! We shared in the beauty of the music together, as one. The boys in the group stood behind us and beat the drums, and they watched us and how we danced, and we felt as though we were the most beautiful girls in the world!

Often I run into women who question their beauty or their ability to attract a mate and they ask me what they can do, and I tell each one to first begin by telling herself how much she loves herself and how thankful she is to be herself! I tell them to do this every single day every time they think about putting themselves down or questioning who or what they are, and soon they will feel it and believe it and live it. Loving yourself is the greatest love of all. I tell them how very beautiful and loving and kind they are and how happy I am to be talking to them and uplifting them in a way to help them to remember what they already know, they are a true gift to this world and a true **diamond in the rough!**

*Everyone is special!*
—JACKIE CHRISTIE

*Think positive thoughts every day.*
—JACKIE CHRISTIE

# CHAPTER 4

# Strength, Courage and Wisdom

*Strength, courage and wisdom are the true essence of a woman.*
—JACKIE CHRISTIE

**STRENGTH:** We women have proven time and time again that we are strong and resilient. We carry the weight of the world on our shoulders, as we step one foot at a time through life's jungle of chaos, all the while wearing a smile on our faces. We have shown many times that a woman's strength is often overlooked or under estimated. The sheer diligence with which we raise our children and how we take care of the home and of our mates prove that we are a force to be reckoned with. There is no way to doubt a woman's worth or her ability to get the job done!

When the going gets tough, a woman gets tougher! When she is called upon to stand or fall, a woman once again proves herself a warrior.

**COURAGE:** Courage really doesn't come that easily to most of us, but it can be gained. A woman will often find herself in awkward situations, and she must still perform. Each of us has to face whatever fear is there and overcome it. Then just begin with small steps and remind ourselves that we can do it if we just keep trying and giving it our best!

**WISDOM:** This is a virtue in and of itself, a gift that many seek and few find. A wise person is a gifted person, a seeker of knowledge beyond self, and beyond the accepted. A wise woman is a *beautiful* woman, a soulful and intelligent woman. She seeks knowledge beyond self, and we can all be her. All we have to do is want to be!

## A SHORT STORY

There was once an old woman who lived in a shack. She had the tedious job of caring for a wealthy couple on their 10,000-acre estate. She worked for them for 25 years, all the while she never once complained. When they asked her to cook and clean and care for visitors well into the night, she proceeded to do as they asked and did so with a smile. One day the wife asked her why she never complained, and the old woman simply replied, "Before I came to work for you, I was homeless. I lived on the street and often had no food to eat, and I prayed every day for the Lord to give me a place to live. I said that even if it was a shack and I had to work to earn my keep, I would do it with honor. So when I met you and your husband that day very long ago, I knew my prayers had been answered and I would hold up my end of the bargain by keeping my promise and work for you with honor."

The wealthy woman was so very touched by the servant woman's story that she immediately told her husband at dinner that evening that they needed to build a brand new home on their property for her, and in the interim she would be staying in the home with them.

The husband asked his wife why they would do such a thing for a little, poor, old, black woman who they only hired to cook and clean! His wife replied, "Because I could have been that poor little black woman myself!"

The moral of this story is the fact the color lines were erased when the rich woman offered the poor woman to live in the family home, and also shows the strength of two beautiful colored girls to unite and share their love.

*Always treat others as you want to be treated.*
—ANONYMOUS

*Beautiful colored girls.*
—JACKIE CHRISTIE

# CHAPTER 5

# Over the Rainbow

As with anything beautiful on earth, the rainbow has long been looked at as one of God's greatest gifts to the world, and I personally agree. Rainbows are full of beauty, love and joy. They are all different shades of beautiful colors! Just like you and I, and all the other colored girls in the world!

We are a gorgeous rainbow of people. We're all God's creatures who share love and laughter. And we are alike yet very different.

We come from many different places, yet universally we are really the same. Just beautiful colored girls! And we should be very proud to be just exactly as we are!

Sometimes this big old world can be cruel and make us question our divine beauty or our place in it, but one thing we must always remember is that each and every one of us has a gift and that gift is our soul. We do not have control over the outside world, but we do have control of ourselves. We can feel good about ourselves and others, or we can just follow what is told to us and never try to dig deeper and find our true essence and meaning.

Many times I have felt the inner twitches of fear and loneliness, and of pain and anger, but I always remind myself who and what I am. I know that being good to myself mentally and physically is my choice and a gift I want to give myself. Life has many challenges for everyone, but I have come to know that all of them are necessary for us to grow and become the person we need and want to be. I would not be able to fully appreciate myself had I not experienced these feelings of helplessness and sometimes even despair.

You see, I too have worn the rose colored glasses, and seen the world through my imagination. I too have chased love and lost. And I too have cried myself a river only to wake up one day and realize that I made a choice to be in the situation I was in, but I could now change it, change my circumstances for the better! I vowed to myself that I would learn from it, and move forward. I would get over *that* rainbow, only to make my own, and the love I was chasing became me. A *beautiful colored girl!*

# Chasing Rainbows
© By Kat Yarnell[4]

I sat high upon the hill of green
watching ivory clouds drift by,
lost in dreams of fantasy
when her flutter caught my eye.

I turned my gaze and looked real close
when much to my surprise,
she crept up on a toad stool
silver tears fell from her eyes.

Oh little one, what makes you weep?
It can't be all that wrong.
She looked at me and murmured
but the magic, it's all gone!

No one believes in fairy tales
or in happily ever more,
they never chase their rainbows
like they used to do before!

The pot 'o gold is waiting there,
just beyond the colors fade,
nestled in a gilded crock
hidden in the willows shade.

But look at me my tiny sprite
I'm not like that, says I...
I'm on the Cliffs of Dover
to watch the dragons fly

She wiped her eyes and giggled
and clapped her hands with glee
her tears turned into silver coins
and she handed them to me.

She flew up on my shoulder
and whispered in my ear
always be that dreamer,
and keep your magic near!

*Believe in yourself.*
— JACKIE CHRISTIE

# CHAPTER 6

# The Executive Order

*I*t has often been said, "A woman's place is in the home." This can be seen as a derogatory comment or as a good thing, meaning the woman is the one best suited to rear the children, and the husband or partner more suited to do the outside work, which provides the means to feed the family.

The world has changed however, and it is socially acceptable now more than ever for women to work and help with the financial part of caring for the family. More and more women are reaching career heights only dreamed of in the past. I'm thrilled for all of us, and for the whole idea that women have a place in all areas of society, and that we are a great asset to our families and our mates and coworkers, as well as to society as a whole. I encourage women to set goals and achieve all that they aspire to, and to never take no for an answer when it comes to your qualifications to do a job, and always continue to learn. 2009 is a year of great change and a historical year in which we have shown how much we've grown as a society and how we all have embraced each other and the idea that change is good and welcomed.

I have a belief that if we all continue to reach out to our fellow neighbors, friends and each other, we will continue to grow and continue to change our ways of thinking and perceptions of each other. We will let go of the negative self-concepts we grew up with and believed, and came to accept as truth. We can start right now by giving each other the love and respect we all deserve, and by helping each other to reach our goals, and uplifting one another.

And I thank Mr. Barack Obama, for establishing the White House Council on Women and Girls:

```
          THE WHITE HOUSE
      Office of the Press Secretary
For Immediate Release March 11, 2009
          EXECUTIVE ORDER[5]

        - - - - - - -

ESTABLISHING A WHITE HOUSE COUNCIL
        ON WOMEN AND GIRLS
```

By the authority vested in me as President by the Constitution and the laws of the United States of America,

I hereby order as follows:

**Section 1.** Policy. Over the past generation, our society has made tremendous progress in eradicating barriers to women's success. A record number of women are attending college and graduate school. Women make up a growing share of our workforce, and more women are corporate executives and business owners than ever before, helping boost the U.S. economy and foster U.S. competitiveness around the world. Today, women are serving at the highest levels of all branches of our Government.

Despite this progress, certain inequalities continue to persist. On average, American women continue to earn only about 78 cents for every dollar men make, and women are still significantly underrepresented in the science, engineering, and technology fields. Far too many women lack health insurance, and many are unable to take time off to care for a new baby or an ailing family member. Violence against women and girls remains a global epidemic. The challenge of ensuring equal educational opportunities for women and girls endures. As the current economic crisis has swept across our Nation, women have been seriously affected.

These issues do not concern just women. When jobs do not offer family leave, that affects men who wish to help care for their families. When women earn less than men for the same work, that affects families who have to work harder to make ends meet. When our daughters do not have the same educational and career opportunities as our sons, that affects entire communities, our economy, and our future as a Nation.

The purpose of this order is to establish a coordinated Federal response to issues that particularly impact the lives of women and girls and to ensure that Federal programs and policies address and take into account the distinctive concerns of women and girls, including women of color and those with disabilities.

**Section 2.** White House Council on Women and Girls. There is established within the Executive Office of the President a White House Council on Women and Girls (Council).

(a) Membership of the Council. The Council shall consist of the following members:
  (1) the Senior Advisor and Assistant to the President for Intergovernmental Affairs and Public Liaison, who shall serve as Chair of the Council;
  (2) the Secretary of State;
  (3) the Secretary of the Treasury;
  (4) the Secretary of Defense;
  (5) the Attorney General;
  (6) the Secretary of the Interior;
  (7) the Secretary of Agriculture;
  (8) the Secretary of Commerce;
  (9) the Secretary of Labor;
  (10) the Secretary of Health and Human Services;
  (11) the Secretary of Housing and Urban Development;

(12) the Secretary of Transportation;

(13) the Secretary of Energy;

(14) the Secretary of Education;

(15) the Secretary of Veterans Affairs;

(16) the Secretary of Homeland Security;

(17) the Representative of the United States of America to the United Nations;

(18) the United States Trade Representative;

(19) the Director of the Office of Management and Budget;

(20) the Administrator of the Environmental Protection Agency;

(21) the Chair of the Council of Economic Advisers;

(22) the Director of the Office of Personnel Management;

(23) the Administrator of the Small Business Administration;

(24) the Assistant to the President and Director of the Domestic Policy Council;

(25) the Assistant to the President for Economic Policy and Director of the National Economic Council; and

(26) the heads of such other executive branch departments, agencies, and offices as the President may, from time to time, designate.

A member of the Council may designate,
to perform the Council functions of
the member, a senior-level official who
is a part of the member's department,
agency, or office, and who is a full-
time officer or employee of the Federal
Government. At the direction of the
Chair, the Council may establish
subgroups consisting exclusively of
Council members or their designees
under this section, as appropriate.

(b)  Administration of the Council. The
Department of Commerce shall provide
funding and administrative support for
the Council to the extent permitted by
law and within existing appropriations.
The Chair shall convene regular meetings
of the Council, determine its agenda,
and direct its work. The Chair shall
designate an Executive Director of
the Council, who shall coordinate the
work of the Council and head any staff
assigned to the Council.

**Section 3.** Mission and Functions of the
Council. The Council shall work across
executive departments and agencies to
provide a coordinated Federal response
to issues that have a distinct impact on
the lives of women and girls, including
assisting women-owned businesses to compete

internationally and working to increase the participation of women in the science, engineering, and technology workforce, and to ensure that Federal programs and policies adequately take those impacts into account.

The Council shall be responsible for providing recommendations to the President on the effects of pending legislation and executive branch policy proposals; for suggesting changes to Federal programs or policies to address issues of special importance to women and girls; for reviewing and recommending changes to policies that have a distinct impact on women in the Federal workforce; and for assisting in the development of legislative and policy proposals of special importance to women and girls. The functions of the Council are advisory only.

**Section 4**. Outreach. Consistent with the objectives set out in this order, the Council, in accordance with applicable law, in addition to regular meetings, shall conduct outreach with representatives of nonprofit organizations, State and local government agencies, elected officials, and other interested persons that will assist with the Council's development of a detailed set of recommendations.

**Section 5.** Federal Interagency Plan. The Council shall, within 150 days of the date of this order, develop and submit to the President a Federal interagency plan with recommendations for interagency action consistent with the goals of this order.

The Federal interagency plan shall include an assessment by each member executive department, agency, or office of the status and scope of its efforts to further the progress and advancement of women and girls. Such an assessment shall include a report on the status of any offices or programs that have been created to develop, implement, or monitor targeted initiatives concerning women or girls. The Federal interagency plan shall also include recommendations for issues, programs, or initiatives that should be further evaluated or studied by the Council. The Council shall review and update the Federal interagency plan periodically, as appropriate, and shall present to the President any updated recommendations or findings.

**Section 6.** General Provisions.
  (a) The heads of executive departments and agencies shall assist and provide information to the Council,

consistent with applicable law,
as may be necessary to carry out
the functions of the Council. Each
executive department and agency
shall bear its own expense for
participating in the Council.

(b) Nothing in this order shall be
construed to impair or otherwise
affect:

(i) authority granted by law to an
executive department, agency, or
the head thereof; or more

(ii) functions of the Director
of the Office of Management and
Budget relating to budgetary,
administrative, or legislative
proposals.

(c) This order shall be implemented
consistent with applicable law and
subject to the availability of
appropriations.

(d) This order is not intended to,
and does not, create any right or
benefit, substantive or procedural,
enforceable at law or in equity

by any party against the United
States, its departments, agencies,
or entities, its officers,
employees, or agents, or any other
person.

BARACK OBAMA
THE WHITE HOUSE,
March 11, 2009.
# # #

*Tell others you appreciate them.*
—JACKIE CHRISTIE

CHAPTER 7

# Proud to be Me

*Beauty is not owned by one woman, but by all women.*
—JACKIE CHRISTIE

ip hop is only for African Americans? Not so! Rock? Why not? I love it! I also happen to love Latin music, pop music as well as R&B. I would say I love all music, and I love all cultures and all people. I especially love all my beautiful colored sisters from all around the world!

You may ask yourself how I can love people I have never even met? Well I can, because we are all the same and you can too! That's the beauty of it.

Because of our many culturally diverse backgrounds we have the opportunity to engage and explore and welcome one another! We can learn so very much from each other. All we have to do is be open to it and that's it! I have found that as each year passes I experience and learn so much more, appreciate more and I yearn for more. I find other people and their history and their heritage to be beautiful and interesting and it feeds my soul to share mine with them.

This world is a wonderful, complex, exiting place and experiencing all that it has to offer is a desire I have every single day of my life! And I want you to feel the same way.

The world is here for our pleasure and enjoyment. All that it asks of us is that we treat it with love, and respect the earth by taking care of the environment and by being good to each other. This is so simple, yet we are just beginning to grant its wishes by making the changes necessary to slow down global warming and to treat this wonderful place better than we did before.

I tell myself every day when I awake that I am beautiful, I'm loving, I'm kind, and I'm so very ***proud to be me!***

From my caramel skin, my curly hair
to my size 9 shoes and the fact that I care,
I'm proud to be me!
You ask yourself, is she tooting her own horn?
Yes, my friend I say, and I wish you'd toot yours!
Black is beautiful, white a delight,
and all the colors of a rainbow are truly a site for sore eyes.
We are all shades of beauty no matter our shape or size!
—Anonymous[6]

**A few tips on gaining self-love and empowerment…**

— *Tell yourself you are beautiful every single day.*
— *Treat yourself with love and respect.*
— *Take time out whenever you need to for your self.*
— *Take time to relax and unwind.*
— *Believe in yourself.*
— *Think positively.*
— *Smile often.*
— *Enjoy nature.*
— *Seek wisdom.*

And most of all YOU'RE A BEAUTIFUL COLORED GIRL, so be proud of yourself!

*A true friend is priceless.*

—JACKIE CHRISTIE

CHAPTER 8

## Girlfriends

"**I Have A Dream**" **is** the popular name given to the public speech by Dr. Martin Luther King, Jr., when he spoke of his desire for a future where blacks and whites, among others, would coexist harmoniously as equals. King's delivery of the speech on August 28, 1963, from the steps of the Lincoln Memorial during the March on Washington for Jobs and Freedom, was a defining moment of the American Civil Rights Movement. He delivered it to over 250,000 civil rights supporters. The speech is often considered to be one of the greatest and most notable speeches in history. And it was ranked the top American speech of the 20th century by a 1999 poll of scholars of public address. According to U.S. Representative John Lewis, who also spoke that day as the President of the Student Non-Violent Coordinating Committee, "Dr. King had the power, the ability and the capacity to transform those steps on the Lincoln Memorial into a modern day pulpit. By speaking the way he did, he educated, he inspired, he informed not just the people there, but people throughout America and unborn generations."[7]

In 1950's America, the equality of man envisioned by the Declaration of Independence was far from a reality. People of color—blacks, Hispanics, Asians—were discriminated against in many ways, both overt and covert. The 1950s were a turbulent time in America, when racial barriers began to recede due to Supreme Court decisions, as well as an increase in the activism of blacks fighting for equal rights.

Martin Luther King, Jr., a Baptist minister, was a driving force in the push for racial equality in the 1950s and the 1960s. In 1963, Dr. King and his staff focused on Birmingham, Alabama. They marched and protested non-violently, raising the ire of local officials who sprayed water cannon's on the marchers and used police dogs to attack them, which included teenagers and children. The bad publicity and breakdown of business forced the white leaders of Birmingham to concede to some anti-segregation demands.

Thrust into the national spotlight in Birmingham, where he was arrested and jailed, Dr. King helped organize a massive march on Washington, DC, on August 28, 1963. His partners in the March on Washington for Jobs and Freedom included other religious leaders, labor leaders, and black organizers. The assembled masses marched down the Washington Mall from the Washington Monument to the Lincoln Memorial, heard songs from Bob Dylan and Joan Baez, and heard speeches by actor Charlton Heston, NAACP president Roy Wilkins, and future U.S. Representative from Georgia, John Lewis.

Dr. King's appearance was the last of the event; the closing speech was carried live on major television networks. On the steps of the Lincoln Memorial, King evoked the name of Lincoln in his "I Have a Dream" speech, which is credited with mobilizing supporters of desegregation and prompted the 1964 Civil Rights Act. The next year, King was awarded the Nobel Peace Prize.

Ladies, let this be a lesson to us all. As I too have a dream that all women can love and embrace themselves and each other. Together we can erase the color lines, wipe out the hatred, and unite as one. My dream is recurring and familiar and I even daydream about it. I pray that we can all live in love and togetherness, and accept that we are truly one beautiful society of great people and wonderful souls. We have so much to be proud of and thankful for. We must begin now to make this dream come true that Dr. Martin Luther King, Jr. preached about, and that I dream about! And many of you dream about. Ladies, anything is possible! All we have to do is take action. And continue to be ***beautiful colored girls!***

*Erase the color lines.*
— JACKIE CHRISTIE

*Those who cannot change their minds cannot change anything.*

—GEORGE BERNARD SHAW

# CHAPTER 9

# A Healthy Mind Body and Soul

*It isn't enough to talk about peace, one must believe it.*
*And it isn't enough to believe in it, one must work for it.*
—ELEANOR ROOSEVELT

*I want for myself what I want for other women, absolute equality.*
—AGNES MACPHAIL

Having the time every day to make sure you're taking good care of yourself is not always easy! And it often comes at a price. But this is a price you definitely can afford, because your well-being depends on it, ladies. And, you are worth, it aren't you?

**Mental clarity:**

The first step in gaining mental clarity is to simplify your life by clearing your clutter and setting attainable goals. Meditation and deep breathing exercises are wonderful ways to release stress and clear your mind. You can also set aside time each day to commune with nature, thereby reconnecting with peace and serenity.

**Health:**

Better health is attainable by making positive changes in your diet and beginning an exercise program. You should not join the program to lose weight. Do it to achieve better health. The weight loss will follow once you begin walking and maybe eventually running or participating in other aerobic exercises. If you are not able do much physical exercise, you can still get healthy. I would suggest that you first meet with a nutritionist and get a diet plan, and then perhaps a fitness trainer, if you can afford one. If not, in most cities many public health centers offer nutrition referrals or counseling as well. As long as they are accredited you can benefit greatly from their expertise. They will be able to assess what you can do and map out a plan of action for you. Even simple exercises, performed consistently, will pay off. Every little bit counts!

**Inner peace:**

Want to have inner peace? You can. Start by:

1. **Taking care of yourself**! Be good to yourself. Get a massage or go for a walk. Read a book or just spend quiet time alone.

2. **Self-acceptance:** Affirm to yourself daily positive thoughts about yourself and believe it!

3. **Getting organized:** Nothing feels better than being organized and having the ability to find things when you need them!

4. **Releasing anger:** Let go of past unpleasant experiences and pent up anger and start living!

5. **Relaxation:** Take a moment to just turn off the TV, the telephone and any other room noise, and just relax for a short while each day.

6. **Slowing down:** Slow your life down. Just because society is moving at lightning speed doesn't mean you have to!

Achieving inner peace is yours for the taking. All you have to do, ladies, is accept it!

I struggled for a very long time to find these three things in my own life. Finding clarity is the best gift I ever gave myself. Clarity clears the way for better productivity and inner peace—two very important things for any woman to have. My health was another thing I took for granted. I was a model and always had a pretty fast metabolism. Still, while growing up, I harbored a sweet tooth that could rival any big time sweet eater! I found out the hard way that it would catch up with me. That's when I decided I had to make positive changes in my life that would aid my finding clarity and better health and wellness. Well guess what, ladies? I could not have made a better life-changing decision.

And you can too. All you have to do is want to change your life, and you will achieve all the clarity, inner peace and wellness you desire.

*A smile is the beginning of peace.*
— MOTHER TERESA

*You can achieve your goals.*
—Jackie Christie

# CHAPTER 10

# Her Story

*Here are seven short stories of real women,*
*each of them a beautiful colored girl.*
*Each has experienced adversities and triumphs.*

The true beauty of a woman comes from not just her outer appearance but also her inner being, her experiences as well as her thoughts and feelings. A woman's beauty is made up of so many little things, from the way in which she treats others to the smile she gives a total stranger to brighten their day.

**A beautiful woman is good, honest, caring, and confident. All women are beautiful colored girls!**

I dedicate this chapter to all the colored girls out there with a story. Share these beautiful, successful, strong, inspirational colored girls' stories, and learn that we all have a STORY. Here's to your story, your experience, and your pain. I congratulate you for overcoming adversity and for all of your triumphs!

# Erika Bjork

## — A Beautiful Colored Girl! —

I'VE WORKED HARD ALL MY LIFE. Now, for some, that may seem like a "casual" comment coming from a girl who grew up in the suburbs in a typical middle class family and a private school education. For the most part, I needed nothing. I didn't have to work. But I wanted to work. When my friends shopped at the Mall, I spent summers and weekends learning about ear infections, foxtails and feline leukemia at my father's veterinary hospital. By my senior year in high school, I worked more hours than most of my friends' parents. At 19, I began my first internship working up to 80 hours a week for no or little pay. By my 30s, I considered 20-hour days or 120-hour-work weeks common. I know what you are thinking? Workaholic? Perfectionist? Idiot? Maybe a little bit of all. But I possessed a sense of accomplishment or even exhilaration knowing I worked hard. Maybe, I felt pride in my work when I finished my shift or completed a project. Pride and hard work are qualities I learned from my dad. Another workaholic.

But it wasn't an event, career change or office politics that represented my most difficult obstacle. It was lacing up my tennis shoes. My greatest adversity was running a marathon. It made a 20-hour workday seem easy compared to a 20-mile training run.

In 2005, I cheered a friend in the New York City Marathon. Talk about adversity. I saw runners with missing limbs, blind, older than the City itself, all running with blood, sweat and tears towards the finish line. It was amazing!!! Just watching a marathon is a spiritual experience for me. I decided if they could run, so could I.

I played a lot of sports growing up—basketball, soccer, water skiing, snow skiing. Running, other than to condition, was not one of them. In fact, I hated running. All the more reason this new goal in my life proved to be harder than I anticipated. Like all of my projects, I researched the subject. Read books on marathons. I asked friends who had run their own business. Visited my local Fleet Feet for the perfect shoes. All the preparation in the world didn't prepare me for that first run over 12 miles. It's the mental preparation that challenges a runner more than any course or any injury. Focusing through pain and soreness. Focus through breathing, maintaining pace and energy. Or worst, hours of time just focusing on my thoughts and me.

Running a marathon also takes discipline. Although I worked hard, I wasn't always a disciplined worker. Marathon training meant scheduling blocks of time for runs. My weeks were now planned ahead for diet, muscle recovery and the dreaded long training runs. Considering, I rarely planned anything personal, this developed into the toughest challenge of them all. But it also offered the greatest reward.

Beyond the pure joy of crossing the finish line and knowing I did something so few ever will remains the knowledge I also did something for myself. As women, few of us do. My training was the only time I had to escape from the crackberry and stress. Slowly I started to look forward to my runs…and better yet, enjoy them!

I did it for me. Not for anyone else. I felt better. I looked better. My quality of life was better. Imagine that? Running 26.2 miles put more mileage on my life, not just my shoes. It gave me experiences I can't replicate with a raise or corner office such as getting lost in the middle of downtown Barcelona during a 20 mile training run or seeing the pride in my parents' eyes as I crossed my first finish line. I crossed two more finish lines and currently am training for my fourth marathon, which I plan to run where it all started—New York City.

I work less now and run more. It is not because I have less pride in my work but more pride in myself. Life is a marathon. I can't wait to run it!

—ᚋ—

# Michelle Winston

## — A Beautiful Colored Girl! —

I AM A 35-YEAR-OLD WOMAN of Anglo-Saxon decent. Often times childhood wasn't something to enjoy, but something to survive. I was born premature at two pounds, ten ounces, and my mother was told that I would not survive birth because I was not far enough along for my lungs to be developed. I grew up the only girl with three older brothers; survival was the name of the game. The minor emergency room knew me on a first name basis due to the endless pranks my older brothers would force me into.

I am an eternal optimist. I look at circumstances and instead of seeing a roadblock or a stumbling block I appreciate the situation because it could have been worse. After years on and off, of fending off sexual advances from two of my brothers from the age eight to eighteen, I know that I am lucky, because it could have been worse. They didn't succeed. My first husband was an alcoholic and took his own life on our front porch, leaving me with our 21-month-old son to care for. Well it could have been worse because he could have taken us with him but this one was a lot harder to deal with. For three years I was in a self-destructive mode, drinking heavily. My middle brother came to live with me and then he was out drinking one night and fell from a moving truck and died. I was looking for companionship in all the wrong places, and sinking further and further into depression.

One day I told myself, ENOUGH. I started going to church and reading my Bible and suddenly I didn't want to go to the bar anymore. I didn't want to drink anymore. I had a mouth on me that would zing someone so fast. I would strike first before they could hurt me. That stopped. I had a real heart change that forever changed my son's and my life. For the next two years I got to know God and learned to like myself again.

Then my Father who I did not even meet until I was fourteen passed away from throat cancer. I miss him so bad but I know he is in heaven and out of pain. My grandfather passed away also just a few months later. It seemed like all of the men in my life were gone. In the mist of carrying on with my life after my father passed away, God answered my prayer, of bringing me my husband and best friend to my door. We have had to deal with issues in my family not wanting to accept me marrying a black man, but we have come through it and have four beautiful kids to show for it. I now enjoy staying home and home schooling them to shape their hearts and minds into the amazing young people that they are and will be.

# Jane Hong

## — *A Beautiful Colored Girl!* —

I AM A SECOND GENERATION Korean-American, born and raised in the beautiful Pacific Northwest. Like most first generation immigrants, my parents came to America with hopes and dreams to provide a greater avenue of potential and success for their children. However, along with their passionate will for my brother and I to succeed also came the pressure to bring home nothing less than straight As, making no mistakes during piano and violin recitals, and be accepted to a top-notch university to become a doctor or lawyer some day.

Well, as I remember it—I spent many hours of my childhood running amuck with my older brother, as my parents worked 14-16 hour days. I made plenty of mistakes during my recitals, bearing shame on my face from seeing my mother's disappointment. I did however manage to be a straight "A" student, but a status, which drastically changed as I entered college. You see, I spent my first years in college convinced that I would come out a pharmacist since being a pharmacist was a "worthy" occupation in the eyes of my parents. I wanted to make my parents proud and for them to rest assured that their labor and sacrifices were not in vain; but that desire to be "successful" as my parents understood it was also the bane of my existence. As a result, my grades suffered and I had no motivation.

As I faced the threat of failing out of college and in the midst of some of my darkest hours, I somehow discovered photography.

Or rather, my father's old film camera that had been collecting dust in our laundry room was waiting for me. The discovery was never intentional, but just purely out of a girl's curiosity; I pulled down the camera box, dusted off the lid and opened it to find what I thought to be the most fascinating photographic instrument that would in due course take me through a fantastic journey. Through the support and instruction of a dear friend, I learned how to use my newfound treasure. Eventually, I started to photograph weddings with my friend as his associate photographer and I found the whole experience to be incredibly rewarding.

Then, I came to a fork in the road—I forgot to mention before that as I pursued photography, I continued to struggle with pursuing other careers still trying to satisfy my parents. I somehow convinced myself that being a photographer would not make any money and that going to law school would be the way to go. With grace and upon graduating, I succeeded in taking the LSATS, applied and got accepted. But still, deep inside I knew that it was not in my heart to become a lawyer.

Then, an intervention—I met my future husband-to-be at a wedding, except, he was the one photographing the event. Through his gentle encouragement, he helped me get past my fears of failure and disappointment, and replaced it with inspiration to believe in my abilities to succeed as a photographer. Today, I run my own photography business, married the love of my life, and my parents couldn't be more supportive. I am a girl with no regrets.

—ᘺᘺ—

# Tanya Kersey

### — *A Beautiful Colored Girl!* —

IT'S FUNNY BECAUSE PEOPLE look at me today and I am the picture of perfect health and fitness. By day I'm a showbizpreneur—the founder and executive director of the Hollywood Black Film Festival, a producer, journalist, author and career coach. By night I'm an amateur NPC figure competitor. For the first time in my 48 years I feel free. The road to this place hasn't been easy.

When I was twelve I was diagnosed with congestive heart failure and hospitalized at Mt. Sinai Hospital in NYC for several months. At one point the doctors weren't sure I was going to make it. It's funny when I look back, because I remember that hospital stay like it was yesterday, but I don't remember being or feeling sick. I survived that episode and several other shorter-term hospitalizations.

Ten years later I was diagnosed with juvenile diabetes. The shock still reverberates through my body. At the time I was a budding actress and print model and had my whole life ahead of me. That diagnosis changed my life. I didn't know how I was going to be able to enjoy a career in the entertainment industry with this disease on my back. Having to stop and test my blood sugar, take insulin, and be mindful of eating a special diet on a regular basis didn't jive with the life of an on-the-go actress. It really sapped a lot of my energy. But I found solace in my writing and quickly turned things around, writing my first book, *Black State of the Arts: A Guide to Developing a Successful Career as a Black Performing Artist,* which is considered the "Bible" for Blacks who want to break into acting. That book led me to launch Black Talent News (BTN), a monthly entertainment trade publication in 1994, and the Infotainment Conference, an integrated informational and networking event, in 1997. Two years later I started the Hollywood Black Film Festival, now considered one of the leading black film festivals in the world.

Throughout the 1990s while I was on a roll with starting all of these new ventures, I was in an unhappy marriage and broke. So broke that I had to sacrifice my own health for my kids. Being diabetic cost money in terms of medicines and the special diet, and I wasn't always able to do what was right for me in order to take care of my kids and keep my focus on my business. But I was determined. My heart problems persisted, probably due to the stress I was under, and my diabetes was becoming more precarious.

Then things started looking up in 2000. My businesses were finally flourishing. I had left my husband, and was happily enjoying a now successful career doing what I loved. Then in 2002 the doctors started to warn me that my kidneys were failing and that I would soon be on dialysis. Kidney failure is one of the complications of diabetes. I refused to buy into that. I went along with their recommendation and went to visit a dialysis center. I threw up in the hallway. I told the doctor that dialysis was not going to work with my lifestyle and that I'd soon take myself out rather than suffer through it. They thought I was crazy and recommended a psychologist. But I was determined not to go out like that. I spent a ridiculous amount of money with a holistic doctor, sitting on vitamin and herbal IVs, and disregarding my medical doctor's warnings to stay away from that "hocus pocus."

And to the doctor's amazement, the next couple of years, while my kidneys were still failing, I was not on dialysis. In July of 2006 I was put on the kidney transplant list. I didn't have time to wait seven years for a kidney and since I qualified for a pancreas transplant, which my doctor warned against, I knew I had to take the chance.

Three months after going on the list they called me in for the transplant and on December 12, 2006 I had a very successful double kidney-pancreas transplant. I now have three kidneys and two pancreases, but I am no longer diabetic and my kidney function is fine. And for the first time since I was twelve years old I am experiencing life in a whole new way, without the stress of my medical condition always in the back of my mind.

To celebrate my newfound life I decided to become a figure competitor even though the doctors warned against it because they didn't want to stress my body. I told them that I had the transplants so I could live and that was exactly what I was going to do. I am now strutting myself on stage in a rhinestone studded bikini, six inch heels, at nine percent body fat, and loving it. Through this 36-year life experience I have learned a few things. First, we are all in control of our lives and should never let a doctor tell us what would happen to us, what we can and cannot do. If I had listened to the doctors I'd be miserable and on dialysis right now instead of living life large. Second, in terms of my career as a Hollywood "insider," I've learned that the struggle is part of the journey and once you look back you realize that there was a lesson in everything that you went through to become the woman that you are today.

# *Laura Wright*

## — *A Beautiful Colored Girl!* —

PERSONALLY, WHEN I think of adversity, I remember my experiences of racism in our society. We as a society have to respond to the problems that America faces with racism. Sadly, and much too often, Americans lump minorities all together; "minorities behaving badly *because* we are a minority?" I am saddened that the larger community does not accept the fact that these men's and women's actions are representatives of no particular race or culture. Their decisions were personal ones, the same as every other human acting badly. I am also saddened because I believe such atrocities by people of color are consistently, historically fodder for America's race theories. This racism gives credibility, albeit tainted, to America's racial myths.

Even as we see these hate crimes in our society I learned long ago that character is something that you learn throughout life. The content of our children's character is nothing more and nothing less than the composition of their values. I learned my values from my mother, a woman of God, and my father, both of whom raised me as a child of young age. I learned about courage and the importance of defending your beliefs and if all else fails to look to God for guidance.

It is true that there is a cultural war going on in America, and the casualties are our children. It is not too late to correct that problem. We should begin by telling our children that character is about values and having the courage to defend those values. Tell them that character is about being true to their beliefs even when others all around them strongly disagree with them. Tell our children that it is important for them to be good citizens and that they should demand that their rights be exercised no matter what. Finally, continue the dream that was made by our forefathers and acknowledge that adversity can be overcome, and by doing so, you will contribute to the desire of peace for our world.

—⚹—

# *Tionna Smalls*

### — *A Beautiful Colored Girl!* —

I'M A MEDIA PERSONALITY hailing from the East New York section of Brooklyn, N.Y. Growing up in one of the toughest parts of Brooklyn has not always been easy. I knew at a young age that I had to be different and want great things out of her life if I planned on being successful. In 2007, I wrote an independent book respectively titled, *Girl, Get Your Mind Right!* after I became single from a six-year relationship. During my time of being single, I realized so many mistakes that women made intentionally and unintentionally in relationships and I wanted to help women everywhere to get themselves together.

While self-promoting my book, I wrote an e-mail in first person to the editors of Gawker Media. That smart marketing move impressed the editors of Gawker and they offered me an advice column, which focused on love, sex, and relationships called "Ask Tionna." Ask Tionna caught on very quickly and before I knew it my column was getting over 20,000 unique views and over 100 comments within hours. Readers were impressed with my no nonsense tell-it-like-it-is attitude and creative vernacular. Words like "cat bag" and phrases like "wet ass and Chinese food" made readers yearn for more.

I became an Internet celebrity overnight and my many loyal fans begin to buy my book and read my urban lifestyle blog, "Talk Dat Ish." Unfortunately in early 2008, Gawker Media switched Managing Editors and they decided that the raunchy column didn't fit in with the new direction the site was going in. I was disappointed but I kept on moving forward and I soon started freelance writing for sites like *Radar Magazine*, *Russell Simmons' Global Grind*, and *SLC Outsider* (which earned me a mention in the Sunday's *New York Times*).

I'm also a host on an internet radio show called Talk Dat Ish Radio on Blog Talk Radio. Talk Dat Ish Radio discusses every topic in urban culture and has had plenty of celebrity guests such as model Liris Crosse, Actor Dennis L. White (of notorious fame), Video Director Little X, and many more. Currently, I work in marketing, and promote independent musical acts, am writing a new book on relationships, and working with/mentoring at-risk youth. The sky is the limit for me and I don't plan on stopping now!

—ᏦᏉ—

# Ꭰotti Albertine

## — A Beautiful Colored Girl! —

MY SECOND EX-HUSBAND always said that the stork dropped me at the wrong house. He could never believe that I grew up on a small cotton farm in Mississippi. But I did! There were seven of us kids, and we worked in the fields all summer and after school—hoeing the new cotton to thin it, and when it was taller, clearing the fields of weeds. When winter came we had to miss a couple of weeks of school to pick the cotton. I always hated that. We did manage to have some fun. You know how kids are. There were many trees to climb, creeks to swim and all kinds of adventures in the barn making architectural designs with bales of hay.

My parents had very little education, and my father was an alcoholic. He worked hard and provided for us, but he could not handle alcohol. Once he started drinking, he would get drunk. And when he was drunk, he was pretty mean. I hid out a lot from all the craziness, and became very shy. Reading was my passion and I lost myself in *Nancy Drew* mysteries and novels like *Gone with the Wind*. My mother had no sense of boundaries for herself or for any of us, but I always knew she loved me, and that goes pretty far. For some reason I became a straight "A" student and really excelled in school. I was the first person in my family to graduate from high school. There was no money for college, so after graduation I moved to Los Angeles to live with my older sister Mary. I became the nanny for her three children. In exchange, she and her husband gave me an allowance, paid for some much-needed dental work, and sent me to college.

My first boyfriend, Jeff, was Jewish and from an upper class, Beverly Hills family. His father was a doctor and his mother wore beautiful, expensive clothes; they had a big swimming pool, and his 15-year old sister studied piano and ballet. They looked like a dream family to me. When Jeff took me to his home to meet his parents, I quickly found out how much they disapproved of me. I was not Jewish, had a thick southern accent, no class, no culture, my father was a poor farmer, and I gagged on lox and bagels. He was forbidden to see me again. But that didn't stop Jeff, so his parents took away his car and his allowance to keep him away from me. That's when I learned what discrimination feels like. Jeff and I were not "exactly" the same, but I could not understand what difference that made. It just felt like I was not good enough for them, and that really hurt.

After college I got an office job and began studying classical guitar, piano and classical voice. Then I married a film composer (Jewish and very sweet), went to a fine art school, then design school, later became an art director for trade magazines, and published my own magazines with my second publisher-husband. I have not conquered the art of staying married. However, I have learned to walk the path that's in front of me and have made peace with it. A therapist once told me that my greatest challenge was to know that I could care for myself. I had always worked (no children), but I thought I could not survive alone.

Today I live alone in a beautiful architecturally designed townhouse near the beach in Santa Monica, which I pay for with the money I earn designing books. I love books! I get to make beautiful covers for books and organize the insides to bring out the story that's in there. Everyone has a story or some wisdom to share with others, and I love helping people turn those stories into a real, live "book."

My other passion is hiking, and I roam all over these Santa Monica mountains. When I'm in such beautiful nature, I'm in bliss. I am also blessed with the most wonderful friends and a big, fat, tortoise-shell cat Zoe, who has stolen my heart.

Jackie Christie and I have worked together on five books. How lucky I am to work with such an amazing woman and her beautiful family. I have a great life, and feel so proud and honored to be one of Jackie's "beautiful colored girls".

# Phenomenal Woman
### BY Maya Angelou[7]

Pretty women wonder where my secret lies.
I'm not cute or built to suit a fashion model's size
But when I start to tell them,
They think I'm telling lies.
I say,
It's in the reach of my arms
The span of my hips,
The stride of my step,
The curl of my lips.
I'm a woman
Phenomenally.
Phenomenal woman,
That's me.

I walk into a room
Just as cool as you please,
And to a man,
The fellows stand or
Fall down on their knees.
Then they swarm around me,
A hive of honey bees.
I say,
It's the fire in my eyes,
And the flash of my teeth,
The swing in my waist,
And the joy in my feet.
I'm a woman
Phenomenally.

Phenomenal woman,
That's me.

Men themselves have wondered
What they see in me.
They try so much
But they can't touch
My inner mystery.
When I try to show them
They say they still can't see.
I say,
It's in the arch of my back,
The sun of my smile,
The ride of my breasts,
The grace of my style.
I'm a woman

Phenomenally.
Phenomenal woman,
That's me.

Now you understand
Just why my head's not bowed.
I don't shout or jump about
Or have to talk real loud.
When you see me passing
It ought to make you proud.
I say,

It's in the click of my heels,
The bend of my hair,
the palm of my hand,
The need of my care,
'Cause I'm a woman
Phenomenally.
Phenomenal woman,
That's me.

—⟪⟫—

# CHAPTER 11

# The Tie that Binds

I believe that God gives us the ability to face each new day with courage, wisdom and understanding, knowing that, whatever sorrow or pain we face, He is ever present and by our side helping us to work through it, not some of the time but all of the time.

Most of all, God, gives us the ability to learn about love and He guides us so that we can all move forward towards a greater understanding of humanity and towards equality for all.

In this chapter I would like to share some wonderful links with you about all things "women" for all beautiful colored girls! For we are all linked by a common purpose—to share and love one another.

### http://www.ivillage.com/

iVillage Inc., a wholly-owned subsidary of NBC Universal, Inc., is the first and most established media company dedicated exclusively to connecting women at every stage of their lives. iVillage.com offers an authentic and robust community infused with compelling content from experts on health, parenting, pregnancy, beauty, style, fitness, relationships, food and entertainment. The site's interactive features include thousands of message boards and a wide variety of social networking tools, allowing women around the world to connect, share ideas, and seek advice and support about everything from fertility to fashion.

### http://www.advancingwomen.com/

To all the women who visit AdvancingWomen.com: you're smart, you're committed, you're passionate and you're ambitious. You are the reason we exist … because we are here to support you in all the multi-dimensional challenges of your lives. AdvancingWomen.com provides career and business strategy, tools and resources to support your career, business and leadership goals, featuring our targeted, diversity job board at Careers. Advancing women.com.

### http://www.teenvoices.com/

*Changing the world for girls through media!*
The only magazine by, for, and about teenage and young adult women.

### http://www.meditationsforwomen.com/daily-inspiration.html/

This is a wonderful site to check out every day. Their free one minute meditations are succinct messages that deliver just what you need to know to make the changes that you crave. Each message is designed to encourage you—to provide insight, knowledge, and inspiration—and to remind you to never give up. For just one minute of your time each day, you can learn to maximize your enormous potential.

### http://www.globalfundforwomen.org/cms/

The Global Fund for Women was founded in Palo Alto, California in 1987 by Anne Firth Murray, Frances Kissling and Laura Lederer. They identified a lack of resources for women's human rights causes worldwide as a key barrier to the improvement in the status of women. They decided to establish a new foundation to raise money for women's

human rights organizations around the world. (For more history, see the Global Fund for Women, Celebrating 15 Years, 1987-2002). Their mission is to advance women's human rights by making grants to women's groups that work to gain freedom from poverty, violence and discrimination.

### http://www.womenfitness.net/

A complete online guide to achieving optimal fitness!

### www.womenshealth.com/

This is a wonderful, very informative site that has articles and tips about women's health and beauty issues. It covers cosmetics and health, manicure safety, dark circles under eyes, and brown skin care, as well as other beauty and health topics.

**http://www.womenentrepreneur.com/**
Marking its 10-year anniversary in 2006, Entrepreneur.com has evolved into the most widely used web site by entrepreneurs and leaders in business worldwide. As the leading small business web site on the internet, Entrepreneur.com serves its visitors' needs by creating the most satisfying experience with relevant content, logical information management and ease of access.

I hope you have found this chapter helpful in discovering great places to visit online, filled with exiting tips, ideas, and a wealth of information.

*Take care of yourself mentally and physically,*
*because you deserve it!*
—JACKIE CHRISTIE

# CHAPTER 12

# One Love

*Red yellow black or green, we are all the same!*
—Jackie Christie

*If we have no peace, it is because we have forgotten that we belong to each other.*
—Mother Teresa[8]

# I, Too, Sing America

BY LANGSTON HUGHES[9]

I, too, sing America.

I am the darker brother.
They send me to eat in the kitchen
When company comes,
But I laugh,
And eat well,
And grow strong.

Tomorrow,
I'll be at the table
When company comes.
Nobody dare
Say to me,
"Eat in the kitchen,"
Then.

Besides,
They'll see how beautiful I am
And be ashamed—

I, too, am America.

It would really make someone's day if you were to commit an act of kindness for them and just show that you care. A little love spread around goes a long way in someone's life. Here are some great ideas that you can do to share an act of kindness to someone. And I would love to hear from you about how these made you feel.

— Help the homeless. Volunteer to work at a mission for a day.

— Donate any extra furniture to a women's shelter near you. It will go a long way to help a lot of people to have a place to rest.

— Gift of Books: Give an inspiring book to a friend in need.

— Cook for your neighbor.

— Tell a friend you care about them.

— Mentor the youth; they can always use a good guide to teach them.

— Donate food to a food bank.

— Donate clothing to centers that help people get back into the workplace by providing them a wardrobe for work.

— Tell you parents how grateful you are they are your parents!

— Give a stranger a reassuring smile to brighten their day.

— Invite all the kids in your neighborhood for hot dogs and lemonade.

— Lend a listening ear to friend in need.

— Volunteer at an agency that needs help; there are so many.

— Volunteer to work for the day at a senior center.

— Help an elderly person across the street.

— Got some free time? Offer to go grocery shopping for your elderly neighbors

— Have extra chores to do around the house? Hire a teen group to do them for you, so they can earn some spending money.

The list goes on but you can also create your own acts of kindness and by doing them you are sure to warm a lot of people's hearts!

# I know why the caged bird sings
### BY MAYA ANGELOU[10]

A free bird leaps on the back
of the wind and floats downstream
Till the current ends and dips his wing
In the orange suns rays
And dares to claim the sky.

But a BIRD that stalks down his narrow cage
Can seldom see through his bars of rage
His wings are clipped and his feet are tied
So he opens his throat to sing.

The caged bird sings with a fearful trill
Of things unknown but longed for still

And his tune is heard on the distant hill for
The caged bird sings of freedom.

The free bird thinks of another breeze
And the trade winds soft through
The sighing trees
And the fat worms waiting on a dawn-bright
Lawn and he names the sky his own.

But a caged BIRD stands on the grave of dreams
His shadow shouts on a nightmare scream
His wings are clipped and his feet are tied
So he opens his throat to sing.

The caged bird sings with
A fearful trill of things unknown
But longed for still and his
Tune is heard on the distant hill
For the caged bird sings of freedom.

*Our children are our only hope for the future,*
*but we are their only hope for their present and their future.*
—Zig Ziglar

# CHAPTER 13

# Be the Change

*Oneness is the perfect expansion of our inner reality.*
*Let our heart's oneness only increase*
*to make us feel that we belong to a universal world-family,*
*and this world- family is a fulfilled Dream of God.*
— SRI CHINMOY[11]

By now you have almost finished the book and you can begin to live your life differently. You are in control of your thoughts, views and feelings.

You can make a difference, just by the way you treat other people as well as the way you perceive them.

You can start right now by loving your sisters, no matter where they come from, what color skin they have, what their culture is, or their bloodline.

We are all the same inside. The world can sometimes be cruel but we don't have to be. We can be kind, thoughtful, caring, accepting of other people whenever we want to be. So why not start now?

There will be racial divides in society, but guess what? That does not change the fact that color, whatever the shade, is definitely is a beautiful thing.

Just let go of the old stereotype of a black or minority person as something bad. And let's all be the majority, BEAUTIFUL COLORED GIRLS! Never let anyone change the positive feelings you now have about embracing this new found way of looking at one of life's true facts, and by sharing with others how proud you truly are about being a beautiful, smart, wonderful, caring and loving colored girl. You have grown so much more just by accepting that being "colored" is a beautiful thing!

# Human Family

BY MAYA ANGELOU[12]

Read at the dedication of the Disney Millennium Village[14]

I note the obvious differences in the human family.
Some of us are serious,
some thrive on comedy.
Some declare their lives are lived as true profundity,
and others claim they really live the real reality.
The variety of our skin tones can confuse, bemuse, delight,
brown and pink and beige and purple, tan and blue and white.
I've sailed upon the seven seas and stopped in every land.
I've seen the wonders of the world, not yet one common man.
I know ten thousand women
called Jane and Mary Jane,
but I've not seen any two
who really were the same.
Mirror twins are different
although their features jibe,
and lovers think quite different thoughts
while lying side by side.
We love and lose in China,
we weep on England's moors,
and laugh and moan in Guinea,
and thrive on Spanish shores.
We seek success in Finland,
are born and die in Maine.
In minor ways we differ,
in major we're the same.
I note the obvious differences between each sort and type,
but we are more alike, my friends than we are unalike.
We are more alike, my friends, than we are unalike.
We are more alike, my friends, than we are unalike.

# Resources

## ENDNOTES

OPENING

1. MAYA ANGELOU, "STILL I RISE", http://famouspoetsandpoems.com/poets/maya_angelou/poems/482 (accessed May 5, 2009).

CHAPTER 1

2. Wikipedia.org, "Human Body Composition", http://en.wikipedia.org/wiki/Composition_of_the_human_body (accessed May 5, 2009).

3. Anonymous, "Just One", http://www.inspirational-poems.biz/Hope_Poems/Just-One-Life-poems-on-hope-and-love.html (accessed May 5, 2009).

CHAPTER 5

4. Kat Yarnell, "Chasing Rainbows", http://www.poetryamerica.com/read_poems.asp?id=338364&start=30 (accessed May 5, 2009).

CHAPTER 6

5. Barack Obama, "Establishing a White House Council on Women and Girls", Executive Order, March 11, 2009. http://www.whitehouse.gov/the_press_office/Executive-Order-Creating-the-White-House-Council-on-Women-and-Girls/ (accessed May 5, 2009).

CHAPTER 7

6.    Anonymous, "untitled poem"

CHAPTER 8

7.    *Wikipedia.org*, "I Have A Dream", http://en.wikipedia.org/wiki/I_ have_a_dream, (accessed May 5, 2009).

CHAPTER 10

8.    Maya Angelou, "Phenomenal Woman" http:// famouspoetsandpoems.com/poets/maya_angelou/poems/492 (accessed May 5, 2009).

CHAPTER 12

9     Mother Teresa, quote, http://www.brainyquote.com/quotes/ quotes/m/mothertere107032.html (accessed May 5, 2009).

10.   Langston Hughes, "I, Too, Sing America", http:// famouspoetsandpoems.com/poets/langston_hughes/ poems/16945 (accessed May 5, 2009).

11.   Maya Angelou, "I know why the caged bird sings" http:// famouspoetsandpoems.com/poets/maya_angelou/poems/494 (accessed May 5, 2009).

CHAPTER 13

12.   Sri Chinmoy, "Oneness", http://www.poetseers.org/ the_poetseers/sri_chinmoy/library/sri_chinmoy_poems/9 (accessed May 5, 2009).

13.   Maya Angelou, "Human Family" http://www.afropoets.net/ mayaangelou12.html (accessed May 5, 2009).

*Never give up on yourself.*
—JACKIE CHRISTIE

*God grant me the serenity*
*To accept the things I cannot change;*
*Courage to change the things I can;*
*And wisdom to know the difference.*
*Living one day at a time;*
*Enjoying one moment at a time;*
*Accepting hardships as the pathway to peace;*
*Taking, as He did, this sinful world*
*As it is, not as I would have it;*
*Trusting that He will make all things right*
*If I surrender to His Will;*
*So that I may be reasonably happy in this life*
*And supremely happy with Him*
*Forever and ever in the next.*
—REINHOLD NIEBUHR

*You are worth it!*
—Jackie Christie